## DATE DUE

| | | | |
|---|---|---|---|
| | | | |
| | | | |
| | | | |
| | | | |
| | | | |
| | | | |
| | | | |
| | | | |
| | | | |
| | | | |
| | | | |
| | | | |
| | | | |
| | | | |
| | | | |
| | | | |

DEMCO 38-296

# Light and Sound

Eve Hartman and Wendy Meshbesher

**Chicago, Illinois**

**www.heinemannraintree.com**
Visit our website to find out more information about Heinemann-Raintree books.

**To order:**

☎ Phone 888-454-2279

▣ Visit www.heinemannraintree.com to browse our catalog and order online.

Edited by James Nixon
Page layout by sprout.uk.com limited
Original illustrations © Discovery Books Limited 2009
Illustrated by sprout.uk.com limited
Picture research by James Nixon
Originated by Modern Age
Printed and bound in China by South China Printing Company Ltd

14 13 12 11 10
10 9 8 7 6 5 4 3 2 1

**Library of Congress Cataloging-in-Publication Data**
Hartman, Eve.
  Light and sound / Eve Hartman and Wendy Meshbesher.
     p. cm. -- (Sci-hi: physical science)
  Includes bibliographical references and index.
  ISBN 978-1-4109-3378-2 (hc)
  -- ISBN 978-1-4109-3383-6 (pb)
  1. Sound--Juvenile literature.
  2. Light--Juvenile literature.
  I. Meshbesher, Wendy. II. Title.
  QC225.5.H367 2008
  534--dc22
                            2009003506

**Acknowledgments**

The author and publishers are grateful to the following for permission to reproduce copyright material: Alamy: pp. 13 (Dan Buchmann), 33 (Enigma); Corbis: pp. 18 (Karen Kasmauski), 29 (Tom Grill); FLPA: p. 20 (Silvestris Fotoservice); Getty Images: pp. 14 (Paul Hawthorne), 21 (Chad Ehlers), 37 (Dr. Stanley Fiegler); Nasa: p. 7; Science Photo Library: pp. 19 top (Faye Norman), 24 (Francoise Sauz); Shutterstock: cover inset, pp. 4 (Konstantin Sutyagin), 5 top, 5 bottom (Marinko Tarlac), 6 (Roxana Gonzalez), 8, 9 both, 10 (Jim Lopes), 11 (Jan Daly), 12 (Alexander Kalina), 15 (Doctor Kan), 17 (Kirk Geisler), 19 bottom both (Gabrielle Ewart), 22, 23, 28 (Morozova Tatyana), 30 both, 31 (Jenny Solomon), 33 bottom, 34 (Alfred Krzemien), 36, 38, 39 both, 40 top (Christopher Ewing), 40 bottom (Beto Gomez), 41 (Jonathan Heger).

Cover photograph of a laser show with permission of Getty Images (Michael Kappeler/AFP).

We would like to thank content consultant Suzy Gazlay and text consultant Nancy Harris for their invaluable help in the preparation of this book.

Every effort has been made to contact copyright holders of any material reproduced in this book. Any omissions will be rectified in subsequent printings if notice is given to the publisher.

All the Internet addresses (URLs) given in this book were valid at the time of going to press. However, due to the dynamic nature of the Internet, some addresses may have changed, or sites may have changed or ceased to exist since publication. While the author and Publishers regret any inconvenience this may cause readers, no responsibility for any such changes can be accepted by either the author or the Publishers.

# Contents

Why is there no sound on the Moon? Find out on page 7!

How does a double rainbow form? Find out on page 35!

Some words are shown in bold, **like this**. These words are explained in the glossary. You will find important information and definitions underlined, <u>like this</u>.

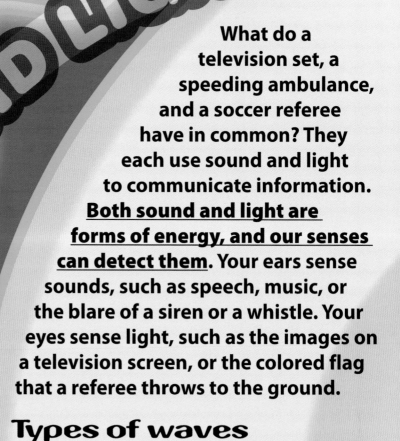

# SOUND AND LIGHT

What do a television set, a speeding ambulance, and a soccer referee have in common? They each use sound and light to communicate information. <u>Both sound and light are forms of energy, and our senses can detect them</u>. Your ears sense sounds, such as speech, music, or the blare of a siren or a whistle. Your eyes sense light, such as the images on a television screen, or the colored flag that a referee throws to the ground.

## Types of waves

When an ambulance is speeding by, everyone nearby hears the loud siren and sees the flashing lights. But how do sounds and lights travel from the ambulance through the air?

<u>Both sound and light travel as waves away from a source</u>. A wave is a vibration of energy. For example, sound waves spread away from a siren. They need a medium, such as air, to travel through.

Both loud sounds and flashing lights tell people to make way for an ambulance.

The flashing lights of an ambulance emit light waves. Like sound waves, light waves travel through air and other materials. Light waves can also travel through a **vacuum** (empty space). This is why light can travel from the Sun to Earth.

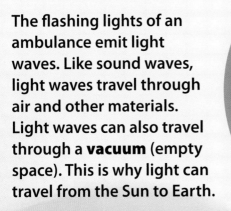

# Fast and faster

When you see a bolt of lightning, how soon do you hear the thunder that accompanies it? If the strike is very close, then you will both see and hear it at nearly the same time. But the farther away the lightning strike, the longer you must wait for thunder to arrive.

<u>**This is because light waves travel much faster than sound waves**</u>. As lightning and thunder demonstrate, light wins every race against sound. In fact, light through a vacuum travels at the fastest possible speed in the universe. It travels at the speed of light (see page 23).

At rock concerts, the music and flashing lights combine to put on an entertaining show. Both light and sound are forms of energy.

A bolt of lightning releases light waves and sound waves at the same time. Because light travels much faster than sound, you see the flash of lightning before you hear the thunder it causes.

# Sound

Pluck a guitar string, and it will make a simple sound. Sound is produced because the string **vibrates**, which means it moves back and forth very rapidly. <u>All sounds are caused by vibrations</u>. A vibration sets in motion the waves that carry the sound.

## Waves through matter

When a guitar string vibrates, the air **molecules** around it start vibrating, too. These air molecules, in turn, make the molecules around them vibrate. In this fashion, the vibration spreads as a wave through the air. The wave is a sound wave.

Sound waves can travel through any kind of matter. This includes solids, liquids, and gases. But they cannot travel through empty space. Sound depends on the vibration of molecules and other tiny particles that make up matter.

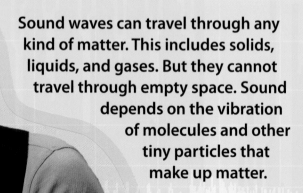

Plucking a guitar string makes it vibrate. It forms a sound wave, which moves through the air.

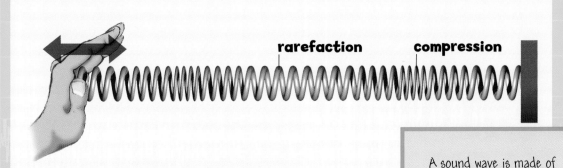

**rarefaction**    **compression**

A sound wave is made of regions of compression and rarefaction. You can produce this kind of wave in a loose spring by pushing and pulling it back quickly.

# Compression and rarefaction

If you could freeze a sound wave in mid-air, you could find regions where air molecules were bunched together. This type of region is called a **compression.** In spaces between compressions, the air molecules are spread farther apart. This type of region is called a **rarefaction.**

<u>**A sound wave travels as compressions and rarefactions move away from the source of the sound.**</u>  As long as the source keeps vibrating, the compressions and rarefactions will continue forming and spreading.

Empty space surrounds the Moon, which makes the Moon a very quiet place. Sound waves can only travel through matter, such as a solid, liquid, or gas.

# TRY THIS

## Feel your vocal cords vibrate

You are able to speak and make other sounds because of **vocal cords**. They are **tissues** that vibrate in the throat. To feel your vocal cords vibrating, place your palm flat against the front of your neck. Now hum a few notes or speak a few words. Compare the sounds you make to the feel of your throat.

# Picturing a sound wave

To study sound waves, scientists often use a device called an **oscilloscope**. <u>An oscilloscope detects a sound wave and pictures it as a wavy line on a screen</u>. The shape of the wavy line reflects the properties of the sound wave. Loudness is a property of a sound wave for example.

The compressions of the sound wave are represented by the crests, or peaks, of the wavy line. The rarefactions are represented by the troughs, or valleys.

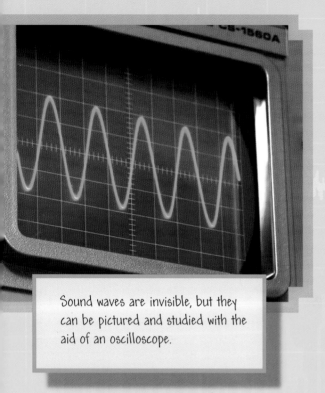

Sound waves are invisible, but they can be pictured and studied with the aid of an oscilloscope.

# Volume

Crash two finger-size cymbals together, and they will make the tinging sound of a small bell. But crash two large cymbals together, and they make a very loud sound.

The **volume** of a sound is a measure of its loudness. The unit for measuring volume is the **decibel**. The volume of a whisper is about 20 decibels. In contrast, the music at a rock concert can be 140 decibels.

# SOUND SAFETY

Can loud sounds damage your hearing? Yes they can, especially if you listen to them all day long. This is why people who work in loud places wear protective earplugs or mufflers.

To keep your hearing intact, pay attention to what your body tells you. Ringing in your ears or a headache are signs that your ears could use a rest. If you are going to a rock concert or other place where the music is loud, take earplugs with you. Even a personal stereo can damage your hearing. So don't play it too loudly.

On an oscilloscope, the height of the wavy line indicates the volume of a sound wave. Loud cymbals produce a much higher wave than the tiny cymbals on a tambourine (below).

## Comparing volume

Volume depends on the strength of the compressions and rarefactions of a sound wave. On an oscilloscope, this strength is shown by the height of the wavy line. Tall waves show loud sounds. Short waves show soft sounds. A straight line shows silence, which is the absence of sound.

low frequency

high frequency

Inside a piano, wires of different lengths and thicknesses are used to produce different musical notes, or pitches. Thin wires vibrate faster than thick wires, and thus make sounds of a higher frequency and higher pitch.

## Pitch

A typical piano keyboard has 88 keys, each of which plays a different note. A musical note corresponds to a specific **pitch**. Pitch is how high or low a sound is.

Pitch is related to the **frequency** of a sound wave. Frequency is the speed of vibration in a wave. The greater the frequency, the higher the pitch. Frequency is measured in units called **hertz**.

On an oscilloscope, pitch and frequency are shown by the closeness of the peaks and troughs of the wave. Peaks and troughs that are bunched tightly show a sound of high frequency and high pitch. Peaks and troughs spread farther apart show a sound of low frequency and low pitch.

## Many speeds of sound

The chart below shows the speed of sound (in meters per second) through different materials.

 Dry air (at 20°C): 343

Water (at 20°C): 1,482

Gold: 3,240

Steel: 4,512

Sound travels 13 times faster through steel than through air. Sounds from an approaching train will travel fastest through the steel rails.

## Speed of sound

Remember that sound waves always travel through matter. **The speed of a sound wave depends on the make-up of the matter it travels through**. In air, for example, the molecules are packed quite loosely. So sound travels relatively slowly through air. Sound travels much faster through liquids, and even faster through dense solids.

# WHALE SONGS

Underwater sound travels roughly four times faster than in the air. In the ocean, whales make deep, musical sounds to communicate with one another. Scientists are worried that noises and **sonar** signals (see page 21) from ships and submarines are stopping whales from hearing one another.

# QUALITY OF SOUND

All musical instruments make characteristic sounds. Even when a guitar, violin, and flute are used to play the same musical note, they sound very different from one another. The **quality** of a sound describes these differences. The differences in sound quality create the wide variety of sounds you hear every day.

## Overtones

Sounds have different qualities because objects can **vibrate** at more than one **frequency**. For example, consider a violin string that is plucked to produce a note called middle C. The string will vibrate mostly at a frequency of 262 hertz. This is called the **fundamental frequency**.

Yet the string will also vibrate at frequencies that are 2, 3, and even 4 times the value of the fundamental frequency. These vibrations are called **overtones**. Although overtones typically are soft sounds, they combine with the fundamental frequency to affect the sound quality.

Overtones are produced at the same time as, but more softly than, the fundamental frequency. Both overtones and **resonance** affect the quality of the sound from musical instruments.

# PIPE ORGANS

A pipe organ is made of pipes arranged from shortest to longest. Each pipe **resonates** at a different pitch. The longer the pipe, the lower the pitch. Some churches have enormous pipe organs, with pipes that stretch from floor to ceiling. They produce notes that are really low.

This is the Chinese dancing water bowl. When its handles are rubbed, the water inside forms waves at a resonant frequency. The bowl resonates with a pleasant sound, too.

## Resonance

A violin is made of more than just strings. The hollow body of a violin acts to **amplify** the sound, meaning to make it louder. In addition, the air in the body resonates with the sound of the strings. Resonance occurs when an object vibrates at the same frequency as the sound waves passing through it.

Resonance makes the music of all wind instruments, including clarinets, flutes, and trumpets. The vibration comes from the lips of the musician. This creates resonance in the air inside the instrument.

# Acoustics

**Acoustics is the study of sound and how it travels.** Scientists and engineers use the principles of acoustics to design concert halls, theaters, school auditoriums, and other spaces where sounds are meant to be heard. They also use acoustics to design quiet spaces, such as libraries and hospital rooms.

## CARNEGIE HALL

Since its first concert in 1891, outstanding musicians from all over the world have been performing at Carnegie Hall in New York City. The main auditorium is famous for its excellent acoustics. Audience members can hear the music nearly perfectly no matter where they are seated.

Yet after the auditorium was renovated in 1986, musicians complained that the acoustics had worsened. The builders insisted that they had changed nothing of importance, but the musicians were not convinced.

After nine years, the musicians were proven correct. A new layer of concrete was discovered under the stage. The concrete was removed, and the acoustics improved.

# Reverberation and absorption

Have you ever visited a house or apartment before people had moved in? Even soft voices in these places can seem relatively loud. This is because sound waves **reverberate**, or bounce off, the bare walls.

When rooms are filled with furniture and bookcases, however, they become quieter. Soft, materials, such as fabric and carpeting, **absorb** sound waves that strike them.

## TRY THIS

# TO BOUNCE OR NOT?

How do objects in your home or classroom affect the acoustics? Work with a partner to find out.

**Materials: Two paper towel tubes**
Tape together an end of each tube so that the ends can open and close like a hinge. Open the hinge to a right angle, and place it against an object such as a book, coat, floor tile, or area of the wall. As your partner speaks softly into one tube, press your ear against the opening of the other tube and listen for the sound. Compare how sounds bounce off different objects.

# THE EAR AND HEARING

The human ear is an amazing, complex organ that allows people to sense sounds. As the diagram below shows, the ear is made of three parts: the outer ear, the middle ear, and the inner ear. Together, the parts translate sound waves from the environment into a message that a **nerve** carries. The brain interprets this message as a sound.

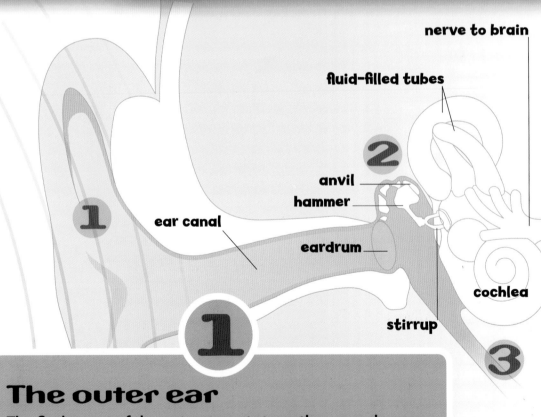

nerve to brain

fluid-filled tubes

**2**

anvil

hammer

**1**

ear canal

eardrum

cochlea

stirrup

**3**

## The outer ear

The fleshy part of the outer ear acts to gather sound waves toward its center. The sound waves then travel into a tube called the **ear canal**. At the end of the ear canal is a thin membrane (sheet) called the **eardrum**. The eardrum **vibrates** when sound waves strike it.

# The middle ear

The middle ear is made of three small bones, often called the **hammer**, **anvil**, and **stirrup**. The bones vibrate with the eardrum and act to **amplify** (make louder) the sound wave.

# The inner ear

A key structure of the inner ear is a spiral-shaped tube called the **cochlea**. The cochlea is lined with tiny hairs. Each of these hairs vibrate at a particular **frequency**. This sends out electrical signals along the nerve that leads to the brain.

The inner ear also contains three fluid-filled tubes, each lined up in a different direction. These tubes give you a sense of balance and position.

## ANIMAL HEARING RANGES

Every animal has a different range of hearing. Notice that the size of the animal does not predict its hearing range.

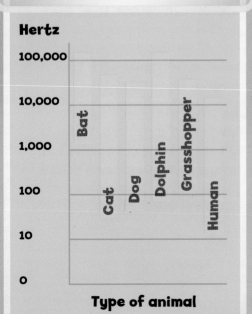

**Hertz**

| | |
|---|---|
| 100,000 | |
| 10,000 | Bat |
| 1,000 | |
| 100 | Cat — Dog — Dolphin — Grasshopper — Human |
| 10 | |
| 0 | |

**Type of animal**

This whistle (circled) is silent to the human ear. But a dog hears the high-pitched sound it makes.

# Loss of hearing

Like other body parts, the ear can suffer diseases and injuries. Often these diseases are mild and temporary. Young children often suffer ear infections that are usually cured without any lasting damage.

Yet infections sometimes lead to hearing loss. So can injuries to the middle or inner ear. This is why you should never stick an object into your ear. One or both ears may develop with defects (faults) before birth.

The tiny hairs on the cochlea are especially delicate, and they often are damaged after many years of use. For this reason, adults older than 70 often suffer from hearing loss. Exposure to loud sounds can accelerate the process.

Can you see the hearing aid that this child is wearing? Hearing aids help people of all ages hear better.

## HEARING AIDS

A **hearing aid** is an electronic device that fits in the ear and **amplifies** sound. Many people hear sounds normally with the help of hearing aids.

Hearing aids once were large and awkward. Today, a very powerful hearing aid may be no wider than your pinky finger. It fits snugly inside the ear canal.

With practice, people can communicate in **sign language** very fluently. Each hand gesture corresponds to a word or letter. Just like spoken language there are many different sign languages across the world. The images below show the hand signal for the letter "L" in British and American sign language.

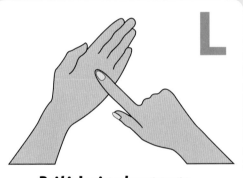

**British sign language**

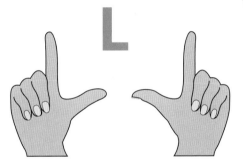

**American sign language**

# Deafness

A total loss of hearing leads to **deafness**. Some people are born deaf, while others become deaf from a sudden or gradual hearing loss.

Deaf or hard of hearing people can communicate by using sign language, which is a system of hand gestures. To enjoy television programs they can read captions of the dialogue (talking). Telephones have been designed that receive text messages instead of spoken ones.

# BOUNCING SOUNDS

A bat spots its prey by bouncing sounds off it. The shorter the time lag of the echo, the closer the prey is located.

The next time you are in an empty hall or visiting a valley, yell "hello" into the distance. After only a moment, you may hear that "hello" again. The repeated sound, called an **echo**, forms from sound waves that bounce off a hard surface, such as a wall or a mountain. Echoes have some surprising uses, both in nature and in human technology.

## Echolocation

When night arrives, bats take to the air to hunt mosquitoes and other insects. But how do bats find their prey in the dark? Most bats do not have very good night vision. Instead they use a process called **echolocation**. As its name suggests, echolocation involves using echoes to determine position.

As bats fly, they release a series of high-pitched sounds. When the sound wave strikes an object, it is **reflected** back to the bat as an echo. By hearing the echo, the bat can tell where an object is positioned.

Other animals that use echolocation include dolphins, shrews, and many whales. And with a technology called **sonar**, humans can use echolocation, too.

**bat emits high-pitched sound waves.**

**1**

**sound waves bounce off an object, forming an echo.**

**2**

**3** **by analyzing the echo, the bat knows an object's location.**

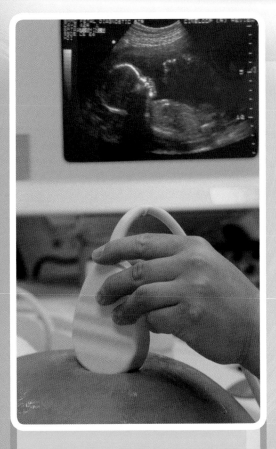

Sonar helped form this image of a developing baby. Unlike X-rays, bouncing sound waves is an almost risk-free technique for studying the human body.

## Sonar

Sonar works just like echolocation in animals. The difference is that a machine emits and receives the sound waves, as well as analyzing the time lag of their echo.

Sonar has many uses. Aboard ships, crew members use sonar to map the ocean floor. Fishermen use it to find schools of fish. In medicine, doctors use a technique that involves sonar to take pictures of the human body. The technique works because different types of body **tissue** bounce sounds in different ways.

# LIGHT

You can see light, but you can neither touch it nor feel it. Light has no mass and it does not take up space. For these reasons light is not matter. Yet light can travel through a **vacuum** (empty space). So what is light?

<u>Light is a form of energy</u>. Light is also part of a spectrum of energy called the **electromagnetic spectrum**. A spectrum is an ordered sequence with a start and end point. The electromagnetic spectrum orders waves by **wavelength**. It includes radio waves, microwaves, and X-rays.

Sunlight travels through gases that make up Earth's atmosphere. It is then absorbed by the rocks and water on the surface.

Some glass is translucent. Although some light passes through it, clear images do not form.

# The speed of light

To reach Earth, light from the Sun travels 146 million kilometers (90 million miles) through empty space. How quickly does it make this journey? The speed of light through empty space is 300,000 kilometers per second (186,000 miles per second). At this speed, sunlight reaches Earth in just over 8 minutes.

The speed of light through empty space is the fastest possible speed in the universe. Light slows down slightly as it passes through matter, such as air or glass.

# When light meets matter

Light travels in a straight path, called a ray. When a ray of light meets an object, one of several things may happen. An **opaque** object, such as a tree, blocks light, which means it casts shadows. A **transparent** object, such as a thin pane of glass, allows light to pass through.

A **translucent** object, such as waxed paper, both absorbs and scatters light. Objects appear blurry and without detail when seen through translucent materials.

# Newton's experiment

A **prism** is a thick piece of glass, typically made in a triangle shape. When sunlight passes through a prism, the light breaks apart into bands of colored light.

Long ago, scientists believed that a prism acted to color sunlight. But in the 1660s, Isaac Newton conducted an experiment that showed otherwise. His results showed that sunlight is made of a combination of colored lights. Each color of light bends through a prism at a different angle.

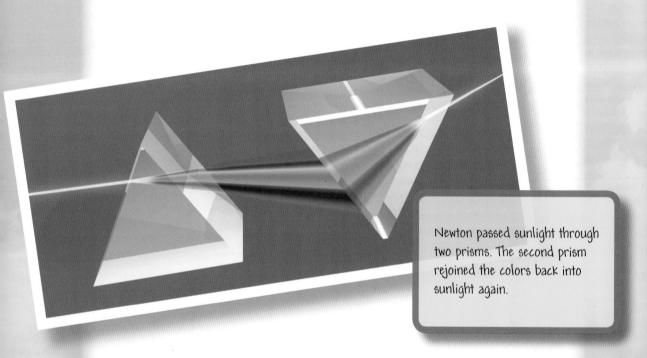

Newton passed sunlight through two prisms. The second prism rejoined the colors back into sunlight again.

# Wavelength and frequency

Like sound waves and other kinds of waves, a ray of colored light has a characteristic wavelength and **frequency**. Wavelength is the distance between two adjacent crests (tops) of a wave. Frequency is the number of **vibrations** per second.

Wavelength and frequency are inversely related. Waves of long wavelength have a low frequency. Waves of short wavelength have high frequency.

# The electromagnetic spectrum

As you read earlier, some sounds have frequencies too high or too low for your ears to hear. Like sound waves, light waves also form at a wide range of frequencies. Visible light makes up only a small portion of this range. The entire range is called the **electromagnetic spectrum**.

Waves in different regions of the electromagnetic spectrum have different properties. Radio waves have the lowest frequencies and the lowest energy. They are ideal for carrying communication signals. Waves of the highest frequencies, including X-rays and gamma rays, carry a lot of energy. They are used in medicine to examine and treat the inside of our body. They can damage body **tissues** if not used properly, however.

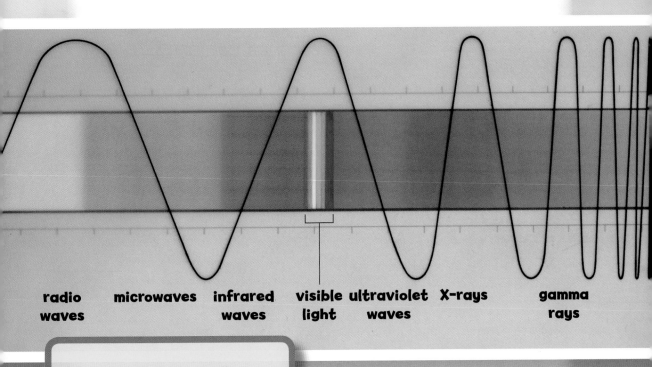

radio waves  microwaves  infrared waves  visible light  ultraviolet waves  X-rays  gamma rays

Your eyes can see only a small part of the electromagnetic spectrum.

# Combining light

The picture on a color television is almost lifelike. One reason is that the screen can reproduce any color that the eye can see.

How can a screen produce so many colors? If you look very closely, you can see that a television screen is made of very tiny colored dots, called pixels. The screen uses pixels of only three colors: red, blue, and green. These colors are called the **additive primary colors**.

Light of any color can be made by combining light of the three additive primary colors. For example, red and green light can combine to make yellow or orange. Red and blue light combine to make shades of purple. All three colors—red, blue, and green—combine to make white light.

A television screen forms an image by illuminating (lighting up) a specific combination of tiny, point-like lights, called pixels. A high-definition television uses over one thousand lines of pixels! The image produced is incredibly clear and lifelike.

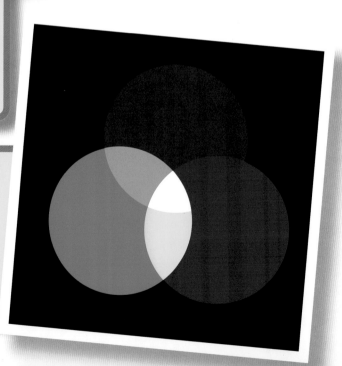

Red, blue, and green light can combine to form all other colors. Televisions, computer screens, and theaters put this fact to good use.

The laser in this cutting tool is very powerful and precise. It can cut a straight line across steel!

7.5"

10"

5"

# Lasers

An ordinary source of light, such as a flashlight, releases many types of light waves that travel in many directions. This is why the beam that leaves a flashlight spreads wider and wider. Eventually, the beam becomes so wide that the light is too dim to see.

Light from a **laser**, however, consists of one type of light wave only. The beam is very narrow and it spreads only slightly.

Lasers are used to read encoded data, such as bar codes and compact discs. In laser printers, they help print images quickly and accurately.

# SUMMARY

❋ Sound travels as waves through matter. Differences in sound waves account for differences in **pitch** and **volume**.

❋ **Overtones** and **resonance** affect the quality of sounds. **Reverberation** and **absorption** affect how well sounds are heard.

❋ The ear uses three main parts—the outer ear, middle ear, and inner ear—to translate sounds into a signal that the brain can interpret.

❋ Light is a form of energy that has characteristics of both waves and particles. It is part of the **electromagnetic spectrum**.

❋ Light travels through empty space at the fastest possible speed in the universe. It slows slightly when it travels through matter.

❋ White light is a mixture of different colors of light. Each light has a characteristic **wavelength** and **frequency**.

❋ Objects appear colored because they absorb some frequencies of light and **reflect** other frequencies.

❋ Mirrors reflect light, while **lenses refract** light. Both mirrors and lenses can be used to form images.

❋ The eye uses a lens to form an image on the **retina**, which sends a signal to the brain.

# QUIZ

**1** A sound wave travels fastest through _____.

A. empty space
B. air
C. water
D. steel

**2** Each key of a piano plays a sound of a unique _____.

A. pitch
B. volume
C. **compression**
D. **rarefaction**

**3** To reverberate means to _____.

A. absorb
B. bounce off
C. refract
D. listen

**4** Red, orange, yellow, green, blue, indigo, and violet are the _____.

A. **additive primary colors**
B. **subtractive primary colors**
C. colors of a television screen
D. colors of the rainbow

**5** What happens to sunlight when it strikes a red wagon?

A. The wagon absorbs only the red light.
B. The wagon reflects only the red light.
C. The wagon absorbs all the sunlight.
D. The wagon reflects all the sunlight.

**6** A telescope can be made using _____.

A. lenses only
B. mirrors only
C. lenses or mirrors
D. lenses, mirrors, or **compound eyes**

# Glossary

**absorb** to take in or soak up

**acoustics** study of sound and how it travels, and the application of this study to architecture and other forms of design

**additive primary colors** colors red, blue, and green, which can be combined to form light of all other colors

**amplify** make louder

**anvil** tiny, anvil-shaped bone of the middle ear

**cochlea** spiral-shaped tube of the inner ear, lined with hair cells

**compound eye** type of eye found in insects, made from multiple tiny, simple units

**compression** region of a sound wave or similar wave in which particles are bunched together

**cornea** thin, transparent structure that refracts light into the eye

**deafness** lack of hearing

**decibel** unit used to measure the volume of sound

**ear canal** tube that carries sounds from the outer ear to the eardrum

**eardrum** thin membrane that transmits sounds from the ear canal to the middle ear

**echo** repeated sound formed by sound waves bouncing off a hard surface, such as a wall

**echolocation** process of using echoes to navigate through an enclosed space

**electromagnetic spectrum** spectrum of energy that includes visible light, radio waves, X-rays, and other forms of radiation

**engineer** person trained in the designing and building of machinery or structures

**fluorescent lighting** light made without much wasted heat

**frequency** speed of vibration in a wave

**fundamental frequency** main frequency at which a sound wave is vibrating

**hammer** tiny, hammer-shaped bone of the middle ear

**hearing aid** electronic device that fits in the ear and amplifies sounds

**hertz** unit for measuring the frequency of a wave

**incandescent lighting** light made from electricity and heat, such as Edison's lightbulb

**laser** light beam consisting of one type of light wave only

**lens** curved piece of glass or plastic, used to refract light and form images of objects. Also refers to the lens of the eye.

**molecule** single particle of a substance

**nerve** thin fiber that carries messages between your brain and a part of your body

**objective lens** lens of an optical microscope that is positioned near the object under study

**ocular lens** lens of an optical microscope placed near the eye of the user

**opaque** describing an object that blocks light and casts shadows

**optical fiber** flexible tube that can carry light waves from one end to the other

**optical microscope** device that uses light and lenses to form enlarged images of objects

**oscilloscope** device that depicts a sound wave, typically in the form of a wavy line

**overtone** frequency apart from the fundamental frequency at which a sound wave is vibrating

**pitch** how high or low a sound is

**primary pigments** colors magenta, cyan, and yellow, which in paint can be combined to form all other colors. See also subtractive primary colors.

**prism** thick, often triangle-shaped piece of glass that refracts light

**pupil** opening of the eye

**quality** characteristic of sound apart from its pitch and volume

**rarefaction** region of a sound wave or similar wave in which particles are spread apart

**reflect** to bounce off, as a mirror reflects light

**refract** to bend an object that is passing through, as a lens refracts light

**resonance** vibration of an object due to a sound wave passing through it

**resonate** produce a deep reverberating sound

**retina** lining of the back of the eye where images form

**reverberate** to bounce off, like a sound wave off a wall or other smooth surface

**sign language** language for the deaf, based on a system of hand gestures

**sonar** device that uses sound waves and echoes to study objects and surfaces, such as the ocean floor

**stirrup** tiny, stirrup-shaped bone of the middle ear

**subtractive primary colors** colors magenta, cyan, and yellow, which can be filtered, or subtracted, to produce light of all other colors

**tissue** mass of cells that forms an organ or muscle in a living thing

**translucent** describing an object that both absorbs and scatters light, forming blurry images

**transparent** describing a see-through object, meaning an object that transmits light

**vacuum** empty space, without matter of any kind

**vibrate** to move back and forth rapidly

**vocal cords** in humans, the tissues in the throat that vibrate to make speech and other sounds

**volume** measure of the loudness of a sound

**wavelength** distance between two adjacent crests of a wave

# Find Out More

## Books

Angliss, Sarah, and Hewson, Maggie. *Sound and Light: Hands-on Science.*
New York: Kingfisher, 2001.

Gardner, Robert. *Dazzling Science Experiments With Light and Color.*
Berkeley Heights, NJ: Enslow Elementary, 2006.

Sayre, April Pulley. *Secrets of Sound: Studying the Calls and Songs of Whales,*
*Elephants, and Birds.* Boston: Houghton Mifflin Harcourt, 2006.

Sohn, Emily. *Adventures in Sound With Max Axiom, Super Scientist.*
Mankato, MN: Capstone Press, 2001.

Solway, Andrew. *Exploring Sound, Light, and Radiation.* New York: Rosen, 2008.

## Websites

**http://www.naturesongs.com**
*Nature Songs: Listen to the sounds of animals, weather, oceans, and much more.*

**http://www.geom.uiuc.edu/education/calc-init/rainbow**
*The Rainbow Lab: Learn how sunlight and raindrops form a rainbow.*

**http://askabiologist.asu.edu/research/seecolor**
*Seeing Color: Discover the science of colors and how your eyes see them.*

**http://www.physics4kids.com/files/light-intro.html**
*Light and Optics: Learn about electromagnetic waves, reflection, refraction, lenses, and lasers.*

## Quiz answers

**1**: D, **2**: A, **3**: B, **4**: D, **5**: B, **6**: C

# Index